The Magical Merry-Go-Round

RUTH MUGRIDGE SNODGRASS
Author

in collaboration with
CATHERINE FITHIAN
Artist

Printed by
GORDON PRINTING, INC.
Strasburg, Ohio USA
2008

Dedication

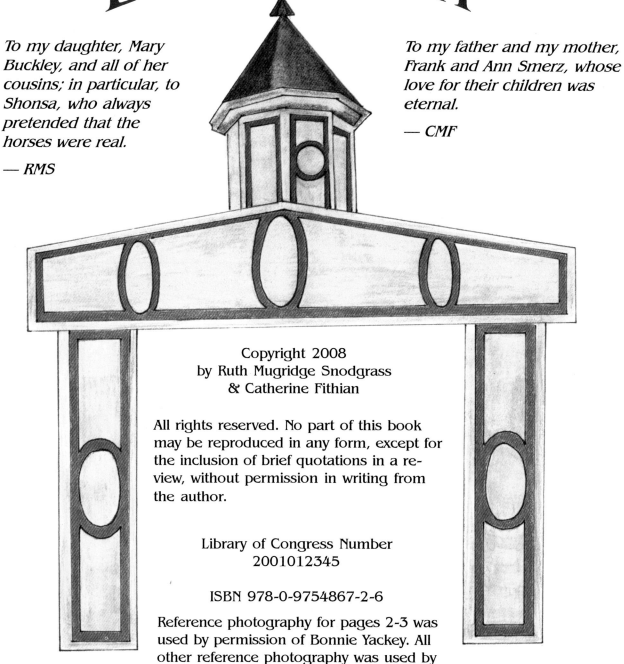

To my daughter, Mary Buckley, and all of her cousins; in particular, to Shonsa, who always pretended that the horses were real.

— RMS

To my father and my mother, Frank and Ann Smerz, whose love for their children was eternal.

— CMF

Library of Congress Number
2001012345

ISBN 978-0-9754867-2-6

Reference photography for pages 2-3 was used by permission of Bonnie Yackey. All other reference photography was used by permission of Mary Buckley.

Ruth Snodgrass is the author of two books of memoir about small-town family life in Somerset County, Pennsylvania: *Dark Brown Is the River* (2004), set in the Great Depression of the 1930's, and its sequel, *On Goes the River*: The Somerset Years (2006), set in the late '30's and the years of World War II.

To purchase copies of *The Magical Merry-Go-Round*, or Ruth's other two books, please email mbuckley2@woh.rr.com. Books also available on Amazon.com

How This Book Came to Be

Ruth Snodgrass of Dover, Ohio, retired teacher of English, French, speech, and dramatics, wrote "The Magical Merry-Go-Round" as a song around 1987. For years she and her sister Gwen had taken nieces and nephews and then her daughter to nearby New Philadelphia to visit Tuscora Park, which the children called "Aunt Gwen's Park." Ruth had noticed that while all of them loved riding the merry-go-round, Shonsa, especially, enjoyed imagining that the horses were real. The song grew out of that observation.

In October 2007, while promoting her two books of memoir at Local Artists' Day at Creekside Nursery in Strasburg, Ruth met Catherine Fithian of Navarre, who was displaying her artwork. A retired administrator in the juvenile attention system, she gives private and group classes at the Linden Tree Fine Art Studio in North Canton. Catherine bought one of Ruth's books, and Ruth signed up for art lessons, even though at the time she was two years over the limit of "Art Lessons for Ages 7-77" promoted on Catherine's business card.

In the spring of 2008, while discussing Ruth's dream of creating a children's picture book around the lyrics of her song, the two decided to collaborate, sharing tasks of composition, drawing, and coloring.

After assembling a group of boys and girls at Tuscora Park before the summer season opened, Ruth asked her daughter, Mary Buckley, to photograph the children, ages 18 months to nine years, on the motionless horses of the temporarily silent carousel. After 200-plus photos they had enough reference material for 28 pages of full-color illustrations, in pen and ink, watercolor, and colored pencils. A second, smaller photo session was held in July. Later, pictures of two additional children, a great-niece of Catherine's and a great-great-nephew of Ruth's, were added, bringing the total number of models to fourteen, including Dave Miller, the carousel operator. A summer of intensive coloring finally produced the completed book, printed locally at Gordon Printing in Strasburg.

Ruth and Catherine hope you find *The Magical Merry-Go-Round* a joyful celebration of the imagination of children and the universal appeal of the carousel.

When I was little, I found a place

Where horses ran with endless grace.

With saddles bright and touched with gold,
What a spectacular sight to behold!

I rode those horses uphill and down
To far-off cities or just to town.

I held the reins, I sat so fine,
So proud, for the world was mine, all mine!

Often I dreamed I was clutching the mane

Of an Indian paint on the Western plain,

Or smiling and waving and unafraid
As I rode at the head of a circus parade.

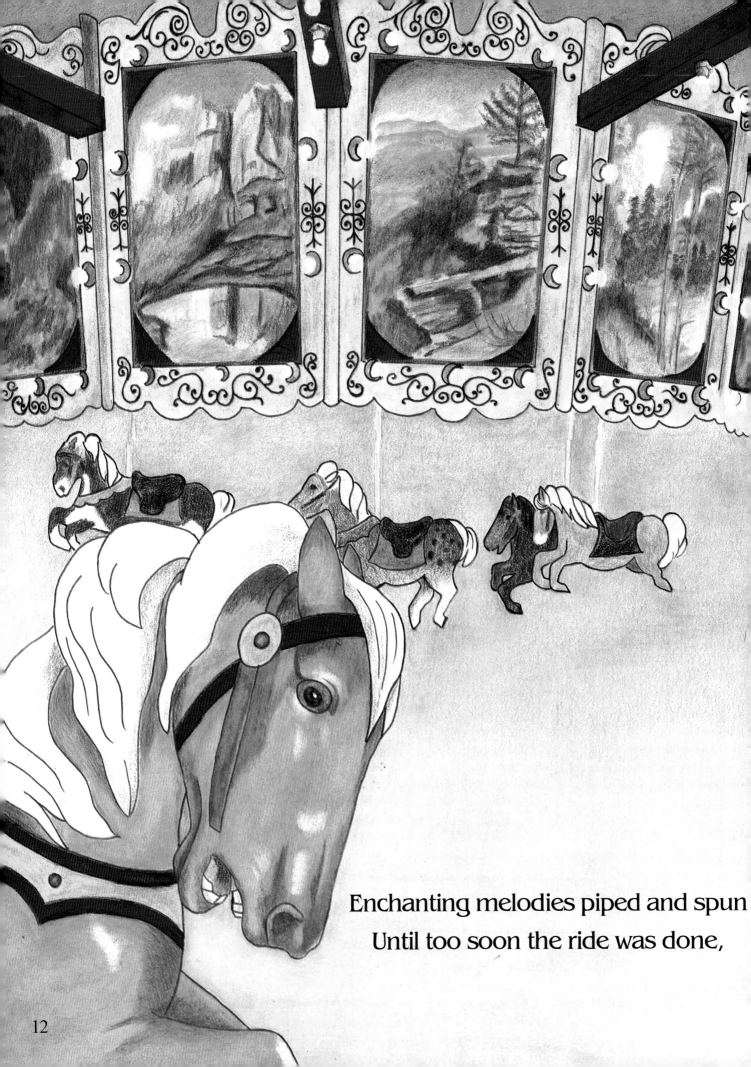

Enchanting melodies piped and spun
Until too soon the ride was done,

And I dismounted with eyes a-gleam,
Still lost in the happiness of the dream.

Imagine the stories those horses could tell
Of children riding the carousel:

Of racing for trophies,

pursuing a quest,

Surveying a kingdom,

or taming the West!

Of trying on courage,

of making a friend,

Of finding the pleasures that come with pretend,

Of galloping, galloping over the ground

On the wonderful merry-go-round, go-round,

ON THE MAGICAL

MERRY-GO-ROUND!

ACKNOWLEDGMENTS

First, we are indebted to Mary Buckley, whose photography provided reference material for the illustrations in this book. Thank you, Mary, for your invaluable work with the children, for editing, and for other technical jobs you performed.

We are grateful to RTY, Inc., and the staff of beautiful, historic Tuscora Park in New Philadelphia, Ohio, home of the specific antique "magical merry-go-round" that inspired this book. Rod Miller, director, has been especially generous with scheduling photography sessions and pavilion events.

We appreciate so much the support of our good friends, Phyllis and Walt Van Horn. Your enthusiasm was most encouraging and your crew of volunteers really outstanding.

THANK YOU, CAROUSEL KIDS! HOPE YOU ENJOYED THE RIDE!

Marisha Gonzalez-Rodríguez, Owen Greig, Alicia Gump, Austin Gump, Emily Gump, Chandler McGrath, Chasse Miller, Sabrina Peterson, José Rodríguez, McKinsey Smerz, Brianne Stantz, Zach Stantz, Keara Yackey

THANKS TO DAVE MILLER,

the only adult pictured in the book, for over forty years of cheerful, tireless ticket-taking. We've enjoyed going around with you, Dave! (Fred Miller's estimate of Dave's revolutions: 1,600,000--and counting!)

FACTS ABOUT THE TUSCORA PARK MERRY-GO-ROUND

Manufactured in 1928 in New York, the carousel is a rare, all-wooden Herschell-Spillman model. New Philadelphia City Council purchased it in 1945 for $3,600, an amount thought exorbitant at the time. Probably the most popular ride at the park, today it is considered priceless.

Thirty-six galloping horses, two hand-carved chariots, and 428 lights are featured on the merry-go-round, along with 18 original oil paintings at the top. Nostalgic music is provided by a Wurlitzer-style 153-band calliope.

From 1986 to 1998 local individuals and groups contributed to the complete renovation of the merry-go-round, including the detailed painting of the horses. In 1988 the Douglas Lee Schwab Memorial Building was built around the carousel, eliminating the need to store and reassemble the carousel for each season.

From *A Tuscora Park Story* by the Tuscarawas County Historical Society